UFO

FRIGHTENING ENCOUNTERS

Compiled and written by
Max Sanders & Tom Lyons

UFO FRIGHTENING ENCOUNTERS

Acknowledgments

It's certainly no easy task for people to discuss their frightening encounters. I'd like to personally thank the many brave people out there who took the time and energy to put their experiences into writing.

Out of respect for those who were involved, many of the following names have been altered or replaced with "anonymous."

Would you like to see your report in an issue of *"UFO Frightening Encounters"*?

If so, all you have to do is type up a summary of your experience, and email it to Tom Lyons at:

Living.Among.Bigfoot@gmail.com

Special Offer

If you submit a report and it is accepted, you will receive an exclusive paperback copy signed by Tom, shortly after the book is released. If you'd like to participate in that offer, be sure to include your mailing address in the email.

Contents

Introduction

It has been a long time coming, seeking and gathering the necessary information to fill these pages. I've spent the last six months contacting a variety of individuals who have had inexplicable extraterrestrial encounters, many of which would be considered frightening. Still, just like anything within the realm of the unknown, it's easy to feel intimidated.

This installment in the series will cover the reports of those who reside within the United States, but I've already started tracking down others who have experienced the phenomena within various other regions of the world. Of course, what you choose to believe is entirely up to you, but the one notion I do urge you to consider is that government coverups *do* occur, and much, much more often than some might think. Of course, it'd be ridiculous to state that the concealment of information only takes place within the subject of UFOs and interplanetary beings. The truth is that it occurs within an expansive array of topics, many that are enticing and many that are quite monotonous but are executed for bureaucratic purposes.

You see, some may choose to believe otherwise, but I firmly reckon that the intent is to aid society to function productively. Let's face it—if any hegemony were to come out and officially declare that they've somehow interacted with intergalactic lifeforms, it would undoubtedly spike chaos, not within *all*, but *many*. In my opinion, it's not all that unjust for government officials to think that certain things should be withheld from many of our citizens. Now, don't get me wrong; I long for much more transparency within government, especially when so, so many of our hard-earned tax dollars fund administrative endeavors.

Unfortunately, wherever there are large sums of money, corruption thrives, provoking tension, distrust, and hatred amongst many of whom would love nothing more than to be able to focus only on all the things that we have to be grateful for.

If you took some time to investigate what's truly out there, you'd quickly get the impression that an overwhelming amount of allegedly "mythical" or "fictional" entities do indeed exist. Isn't it intriguing to consider how there are millions of living people at this very moment who are fully aware of things that would blow your mind?

The next time that you find yourself immersed within an urban environment, I'd like you to take a few moments to consider each of the individuals that you pass. I don't possess an ounce of doubt that a surprising number of these pedestrians have had encounters or experiences that would utterly astonish you and would unravel various aspects that modern society has instilled within your outlook on life. I should probably mention that I don't intend to insult any of my readers; for all I know, there's a damn good chance that *you* may very well possess knowledge that goes a great deal deeper than everything I've been able to ascertain thus far. Although these notions might be obvious to some, I think it's considerate to bring them up for those who are on the fence. This could pertain to those who have recently endured unexplainable phenomena, or those who have had a hunch that there is so much more to this existence than what the authorities and mainstream science tell us.

How did I find myself enthralled in this subject matter? Well, as you might've expected, I too have experienced alien contact. To be frank, it took me a significant amount of time to accept it and, in a sense, move on from it. Eventually, a close friend recommended that a useful method for dealing with trauma is to write your thoughts down. Though I was skeptical at first, I can recall immediately feeling some sense of relief after jotting down only the first few sentences of my experiences.

I then became enticed by this therapeutic effect, and after completing the narrative of my encounter, I longed for more; I came up with the idea to seek others who claimed to have undergone similar circumstances and asked them if I could be their personal ghostwriter. I'd be lying if I said I hadn't gotten rejected more than once; however, I was quickly encouraged to learn just how many people out there were willing to share these stories with the rest of humanity. Many of these abductees instantly declared their desire to remain anonymous; for the sake of protecting these identities, I decided it would be best to provide aliases to all of the individuals within this content. To give the individual accounts a personable tone, Tom Lyons and I decided that we would rewrite all of them in the first person. I, as well as the abductees, agreed that this would help our readers to become more immersed within the text.

I should mention that I will be concluding this volume with the initial portion of my very own alien interaction.

That account will then pick up at the end of the following volume.

Now, without further hesitation, we will dive into the accounts of people who have come face-to-face with extraterrestrial beings. Enjoy.

-Max

Report #1

My name is Sara, and I was 18 years of age when the incident took place. I grew up in the city of Portland, Oregon, but somehow never managed to embrace outdoor activities such as camping and hiking. I know that must seem strange to many, but I was far more interested in urban entertainment such as dance clubs, movie theaters, fancy restaurants, etc.

I had only just graduated from high school, and my ex-boyfriend, Michael, and I were doing the whole dramatic, teenage tradition of counting down the days until our departures for college would separate us. His school was only a few hours away from Portland; however, I had decided I wanted to experience the east coast since that's where my mother had grown up. As soon as I had received notice that I had gotten accepted into NYU, I think my boyfriend and I both sort of silently knew that our hearts would also eventually embark in different directions.

To this day, I'm still uncertain as to whether Michael intended for it to be a strategy for us to grow closer or a sort of epic finale to our seventeen months together, but he arranged for us to go on an Alaskan camping trip. I was rather quick to turn down the proposition, but he was very persistent, making it seem as though I'd crush his heart if I didn't go. Both of my parents were the laid-back types, allowing me to do pretty much whatever I wanted, so I wasn't exactly able to use them as an excuse since Michael was very aware of their lenience. He assured me that we wouldn't be camping anywhere *too* remote and that if at any point I found myself to be hating the whole tent experience, he'd happily cover the cost of renting a nearby cabin. After a consistent begging, I ultimately complied, concluding that the trip would provide me some interesting material to discuss with my peers at school.

After a few weeks of carefully coordinating everything, the two of us set off on what we had planned to be a 10-day adventure. I can still recall the jitters I was feeling as I sat at the window seat of the budget airplane, wondering what the whole experience would be like. Like many other residents of our community, Michael grew up in one of those families that were often participating in some sort of outdoor activity, whether it be hiking, camping, rafting, snowmobiling, cross-country skiing, etc. Even though his parents were wealthy, it was apparent they received more pleasure road tripping in their bright green Volkswagen Bus as opposed to many of the luxuries that their money could buy. At the time, I was relatively incapable of understanding that, but years later, I began to appreciate the charm of it all. My point is that Michael was very much in his element with this whole adventure, so as nervous as I was, that notion helped me to grasp at least a bit of solace. I'm able to vividly recall the anxiety transitioning into mild excitement as we began our descent among the breathtaking landscape that was now visible from below. I suddenly became overwhelmingly grateful that I had agreed to participate in something so far out of my comfort zone.

Shortly after landing in Anchorage, we rented a smaller sized SUV before heading for a bed-and-breakfast that was stationed just outside of the metropolitan area. I remember thinking that the architecture of downtown Anchorage possessed some similarities to Portland, probably helping me to feel comfortable in a somewhat familiar environment. I have no idea what the name of the restaurant was, but that evening we ate at this popular burger place that offered maybe 20 types of burgers, each drastically differing in ingredients, buns, sauces, etc. By no means have I ever been a frequent consumer of red meat, but the goofy, elderly owner of the place persuaded me into ordering the one that was topped with peanut butter and various other unconventional toppings; it was surprisingly delicious.

The following morning, we set out before sunrise toward the campground, which was only an hour or two away. Due to it being the summer season, the scenery was as vibrant as could be; multiple shades of green and blue stimulated our eyes as we drove toward the mountains with the windows rolled down and the radio blaring. We passed numerous campers, hikers, and fishermen, which instilled a certainty that we were headed for a safe destination. Having grown up in Oregon, I had heard numerous stories of mountain lion and bear attacks, so I was nervous about something like that happening to us. But observing the multitude of happy families helped to manifest a sense of security.

We eventually arrived at the destination, which was at a bit higher elevation than I had expected. The winding roads made me feel a little carsick, so I laid on the reclined passenger seat for a few minutes while Michael set up camp; it's not like I would've been much help anyway. Soon, my nausea passed, enabling me to exit the vehicle and embrace our beautiful surroundings. To say the campground was serene would be an understatement; it was positioned only yards away from the clearest of rivers that ran deep into a mountainous horizon. The temperature was near perfect with a slight breeze in the air. The only thing at the time that remotely concerned me was the lack of other people, but Michael assured me that others had to be nearby as we were occupying an area that was said to be an "open secret" among avid campers. I couldn't help but feel a tad uneasy because of this, but I was then relieved when a caravan of kayakers paddled down the river, joyfully waving as they noticed us near the water's edge.

The next couple of days were fantastic, filled with mild hiking trails, frisbee throwing, reading, napping, fishing, etc. I noticed that my anticipation for danger was simmering as time went on, growing more acquainted with my surroundings and the overall rhythm of outdoor adventuring. Sleeping in the tent was somewhat nerve-wracking the first night; there were so many sounds that I was unfamiliar with; however, observing Michael's calm demeanor helped to stifle my unnecessary paranoia.

It was either the third or fourth day when we decided to go for a late morning swim. It rained the previous night and into the early morning, and I can vividly recall feeling the sensation of thick, wet grass beneath my toes as I walked toward the river. Michael and I playfully splashed around in the water before using some kind of organic shampoo to wash our unkempt hair. We were just about to exit the river when Michael noticed a muscular buck on the other side of the river, opposite to where our camp was situated. Our admiration quickly went awry when we simultaneously saw that something about the animal wasn't right. The deer timidly approached the water's edge, coming close enough for us to observe a sight that I will never, ever forget; it was missing its lower mandible.

My initial assumption was that it had to have been in some sort of scuffle with a predator or perhaps a rival buck; however, Michael brought the absence of blood to my attention. It made no sense. If the poor animal had been attacked by a predator such as a mountain lion, wouldn't there be heavy bleeding? This buck didn't even appear to be fatigued; honestly, it looked to be relatively healthy, aside from its missing jaw.

I remember asking Michael if it could've been attributed to some kind of disease or birth defect, but he shook his head. He brought it to my attention how there's no way this animal could've survived without the ability to chew and consume food; it'd be surprising if the thing could even last more than 24 hours in its current state. Whatever had happened to it must've taken place very recently. He went on to explain his theory that this could've *only* been the result of some sort of precision surgery.

I remember my mind racing as it attempted to make sense of it all, but no success. Even if there were, say, a group of active zoologists out here, why on earth would they carefully remove the lower jaw from a creature and then set it free?

Having pondered the bizarre occurrence for more than a few minutes, the two of us began to exit the water. After leaving the river, we both turned to take one more look at the strange deer, but it was no longer visible. I'd be lying if I were to say I didn't feel a bit peculiar the rest of the day. Michael seemed to carry on, being able to disregard the encounter. I was having so much fun beforehand that I tried my best to shake it, but it was no use; my memory persisted in painting the ominous image.

I had a tremendous amount of trouble falling asleep that night, frequently tossing and turning on a queen-sized air mattress. It was maybe around 12:30 am when I perceived a faint light off to my left side and through the wall of the tent. Although it didn't appear to be very close, it was still bright enough to cause further disturbance to my already tarnished rest. My initial reaction was that it must be another group coming to set up camp at a nearby spot; it was extremely late to be doing so, but perhaps they had gotten sidetracked and were behind schedule? Already irritated due to my lack of sleep, I poked my head outside to see what was going on. Michael momentarily woke to ask what I was doing, but instantly fell back asleep. The environment was so quiet that I could've sworn the sound of the zipper echoed for miles.

The clear, starlit sky enabled great lucidity across the landscape. While standing with one foot still inside the tent, I looked to my left toward the light. I can only describe what I saw as a ball of light, or an *orb*, as I later discovered is a term preferred by many. The distance made it too difficult to estimate the size or even discern any mechanism that projected it. Slightly dumbfounded as to what I was looking at, I decided to wave my hand above my head with the hopes that someone over there may notice that other campers were nearby and might redirect the light as an act of courtesy.

Due to a lack of voices, I had begun to assume that it was most likely just one camper who had maybe grown tired on their journey and decided to pull over so that they could lay out their sleeping bag or something. It was about ten seconds after I waved my hand that the light switched off, rendering my pupils incapable of depicting anything within that area. Now beginning to get creeped out, I hurried back inside the tent with the hopes of being able to get some rest finally. It wasn't long before my senses were interrupted by the same light. However, I barely had any time to react before I watched the light (through the sidewall of the tent) slowly but silently rise before it quickly flew across a section of the sky that was almost directly above our tent.

Utterly perplexed by what I had just seen, I nudged Michael more than a few times, waking him from the deep sleep that I now envied. After elaborating on what I witnessed, he didn't seem to acknowledge it with any real intrigue, quickly lowering his head back to the pillow. It couldn't have been any more than a couple of minutes before the entire area illuminated with soft glimmer. This time I didn't need to wake Michael, as he was quick to rise from the inflatable mattress before I could take any action. The two of us swiveled our heads in all directions, utterly clueless as to what could be causing the luminescence. Aside from the faint sound of the running water from the nearby stream, everything seemed to be silent. All of this took place well before fully-electric vehicles had come into existence, so neither of us possessed the slightest speculation that that could be what was responsible; we both knew something extraordinary was among us.

We must've remained still for a few minutes, nearly speechless, desperate for any kind of noise that would hint toward whatever it was that was now almost certainly just outside our tent. I remember it so well as I whispered, "who do you think is out there?" only to be instantly silenced by the appearance of a silhouette. The thing suddenly appeared and then glided across the space that was visible through the right wall of the tent. It then seemed to merge with the glowing light.

Chills traveled up and down my spine as soon as it occurred to me that Michael was trembling; his usual confident and composed demeanor had faded, as he was unable to develop any possible explanation for what was taking place. Seeing him in a state of panic for the first time was enough to prompt my confusion to transform into terror. Our heads shifted focus as we spotted another silhouette that appeared within the space that was visible through the entrance side of the tent. The most peculiar aspect of the sight was that the entity seemed to be steadily gliding around a portion of the landscape in a figure-eight pattern. I can vividly recall clutching the fleece blanket within my shaking hands while both Michael and I nervously waited for any kind of relieving clarification. The incident continued for a few more minutes as we whispered to one another. The light then suddenly went out, and the silhouette of the slim figure was no longer visible from within the tent.

Neither of us was able to comprehend what followed, but it wasn't long before the morning sunshine greeted us, as well as the sound of birds chirping. We both felt mild nausea as we discussed the event, quickly establishing that it was anything but a dream.

Perpetually disturbed by the mystery of it all, we left the campground and spent the remainder of our trip at a hotel in downtown Anchorage before boarding our flight back to Oregon.

As I had expected, Michael and I split during our freshman year at college. We never again discussed the event.

-Submitted by Sara R.

Report #2

My friends call me Jim. My younger brother and I spent a substantial portion of our childhood moving from state to state under the care of my single mother, who often had to relocate due to her position at Toyota. My brother and I hated how we regularly had to leave our friends and acquire new ones. Mom would continuously reassure us that it was only a matter of time until she'd be in a position where we could establish a more permanent home.

I was 16 years old when we were eventually able to settle within Charleston, South Carolina. My mother made this decision because the city was only about an hour away from my grandfather's farm (my grandmother had passed away a few years before our move). Even though the property was still a functioning farm, my grandpa's participation had minimized over the years; he mostly just monitored the handful of workers that he and my grandmother had employed decades earlier. Anyway, I never had all that much interest in going to college, so after graduating from high school. Mom convinced me to spend the summer working at the farm, earning a bit of money while simultaneously gaining some experience for future endeavors.

Also, it was clear that Mom thought this would be a prime opportunity for me to spend time with Grandpa and get to know him better. It had to have been the second or third week in June of 2001 that me, Mom, my brother, and Mom's new boyfriend headed Northwest to the desolate but gorgeous property. Upon our arrival, Mom was quick to display her concern for the apparent dilapidation of the place we once knew to be well-maintained and thriving with crops. Shortly after entering the house and greeting my grandfather, it was further discernible to my mother that something wasn't quite right. My detail-oriented Grandfather certainly wasn't one to allow things to fall apart; after all, this is

how the farm managed to be such a
profitable business for so many years,
providing my mother and her siblings
with a storybook upbringing. Of course,
we were all quick to credit it to some
sort of dementia, or whatever other
possible mental illness. We later came to
find out that he had been sporadically
firing the workers over the last few
months, leaving only two or three to
take on the extensive list of required
duties. His character *did* seem different
to me, but it was difficult to pinpoint
whether it was a side effect of aging or
the fact that business was slowing, thus
leaving him no choice but to make a few
undesirable changes. Either way, it was
quite clear that he had little interest in
discussing any of it.

The initial plan was for all of us to
come for a long weekend visit, but then

I'd be left behind to learn the ways of the farm. To say the trip immediately felt awkward would be to put it lightly. It was the first time that Grandpa had met Mom's latest boyfriend, but it came off like he didn't even want to acknowledge the guy. Eventually, the weekend passed, and the lousy energy persisted until the three of them had to depart. I can remember Mom asking me multiple times whether I still wanted to stick around. I assured her that everything would be fine and that I'd call her in a few days.

Aside from learning how the place functioned—especially considering the possibility that I could one day take it over—it was important to me that I gained some sense for what was on Grandpa's mind. Honestly, I had never seen the man when he wasn't in a joyful state; to my perception, you could say it clashed with the laws of the universe.

The following day I set my alarm to wake just before sunrise. Expecting Grandpa to be awake and hard at work, I threw on a pair of worn denim pants and an old t-shirt. It was almost immediately after I exited the guest bedroom that I caught notice of deep, continuous snoring originating from my grandfather's room. Somewhat surprised that I had beaten him to the punch, I poured myself a glass orange juice before venturing outside to see whether there any tasks I could tend to.

The beautiful light from the sunrise and fresh morning air was an instant reminder as to why I was drawn to that kind of work. I was one of those folks who was always attracted to physical labor as opposed to an office job. I had a real passion for being outside, and the whole idea of farming just seemed to click with me from a young age.

After noticing that a couple of the worker's vehicles were parked in the driveway, I headed for the stable to greet the horses and to see if I could be of any assistance. A younger man who went by the name of Iggy was there and was quick to introduce himself. Even though I had somewhat frequently visited the place while growing up, it was always during holidays, so I rarely got to see the place in action, as most employees were absent at those times.

After getting to know Iggy a bit, I eventually grew comfortable in asking him whether he noticed anything different about my Grandpa lately. With a voice of concern, he responded that the man hadn't been himself for a matter of months. It was to Iggy's perception that Grandpa's character began to alter almost immediately following the disappearance of some of the livestock. That was the first time I had heard of this, and I was unsure whether he was implying that they were escaping, dying, stolen, eaten by predators, etc.

Iggy also explained that animals had been vanishing in the middle of the night, without any trace. It wasn't long before Grandpa had heavy-duty locks installed on many of the shelters, but those quickly proved to be no use; the numbers still diminished throughout the night even though all of the locks were fully intact the following morning.

Nobody was able to make any sense of the phenomenon, and it then persuaded Grandpa to take it to the next step and install surveillance cameras within multiple sections of the farm that encompassed the livestock. For whatever reason, the camera setup seemed to briefly deter whatever it was that was happening to these animals, allowing Grandpa to feel some relief. However, it was no more than two or three days before the vanishings began to occur again. But when Grandpa reviewed the surveillance footage, he was baffled to see that the footage would turn static at random times throughout the night.

The unexplainable happenings began to create tension between Grandpa and the employees that he once trusted. He couldn't reach any sort of conclusion other than that at least of the workers were going behind his back and, I suppose, stealing the animals for profit. Grandpa interrogated many of the workers, firing a few while others decided to quit.

Grandpa then took it to the next level by hiring someone to monitor the farm during all hours of the night and catch the perpetrators. Mysteriously, the watchman abandoned the duty the very first night, insisting that the place was cursed.

These events had created quite a distraction; thus, a backlog of work had begun to pile up. Once loyal customers were now questioning the holdup, all while Grandpa seemed to grow more cynical. My inquiry wasn't the first time Iggy was approached about what was going on. Seeing as how he was now considered to be one of the veteran employees, it wasn't rare that he found himself dealing with client relations. I bet that was pretty awkward for him because he had a calm demeanor and never really knew what to use for a logical explanation.

It got to the point where he'd stop asking Grandpa what to tell the concerned folks because it always seemed to make him crabby and lash out about several things, completely failing to reach any kind of productive solution. Iggy told me how he had offered more than once to stick around through the night to see if he could uncover what was going on, but Grandpa developed the strict policy that he didn't want any of the workers near the property past the evening hours. Fortunately, the livestock disappearances *did* cease, but strangely enough, Grandpa's personality never returned to what it once was.

It had maybe been a month since I had arrived at the farm and first discussed the situation with Iggy. I spent the next hour or so tending to the horses, becoming acquainted with their routines, and how to provide them with optimal care. I got so caught up with everything that I was learning that it dawned on me how I still had yet to greet Grandpa. After giving the heads up to Iggy, I whisked the sweat from my face and walked the path that led back toward the main house.

Almost immediately after entering the doorway, I heard what sounded like mumbling coming from Grandpa's bedroom. As I got closer to the door, I perceived what sounded like panic-induced yelps and mumbled speech. Out of sheer concern for his wellbeing, I couldn't help but impulsively burst through the doorway to ask if he was alright. The site rendered me speechless. I know this is incredibly hard to believe, but my grandfather's body levitated about a foot above the mattress. He was facedown, similar to how you would lie on a massage table.

My grandpa continued to mutter a series of words before his head eventually turned to the side and faced me. His eyes remained closed for another five or so seconds before he quickly fell to the mattress, immediately opening his eyes. He asked me what the hell I was doing in there, but before I even had the chance to respond, he shouted at me to get out. I asked him repeatedly to help me understand what I had just witnessed, only to be interrupted by more hollering. It was a bit later when he walked through the kitchen, and I noticed what looked like four, tiny, evenly spaced puncture marks, nestled into the back of his neck just below the hairline. I did all I could to try to get him to talk, but he was relentlessly stubborn and wouldn't have it. He commanded me to head outside to find one of his employees, Maria, and assist her with the spreading of fertilizer. Another thing I'll never forget is how he yelled out to me as I was opening the screen door, "if you ever want to take over the farm, you'll learn some respect!"

None of what had just taken place made even the slightest bit of sense to me. I stepped back outside and pondered whether I should inform Iggy of what I had recently seen. But it seemed so challenging to come up with the appropriate words as not to sound like I wasn't playing some kind of twisted prank.

Anyway, I did as Grandpa instructed; after introducing myself to Maria, I spent the next few hours baking in the sun while scattering fertilizer throughout the seemingly endless stretch of soil. It was either that she wasn't all that fluent in English, or she just wasn't interested in conversing with me, but it felt evident right from the introduction that I wasn't going to have any luck discussing the bizarre occurrence.

Much to my surprise, I caught notice of Mom's voice, calling out to me as she approached from the distance. As she neared, she informed me that Grandpa had called her earlier and said that he no longer wanted any visitors at the farm. He didn't give much of an explanation, but Mom was quick to grant him his wish. Before departing, Grandpa gave me a firm handshake, looked me straight in the eyes, then murmured, "I wish you could understand."

That would end up being the last time I ever saw my grandfather, as well as the farm. It's taken me many years to accept the reality of everything that happened during that strange time, but I believe that it influenced me to be a much more open-minded individual. And it's because of that, that I'm able to get along with most people I meet, especially the ones who have also experienced strange phenomena.

-Submitted by James Livingston

Are you enjoying the read?

I have decided to give back to the readers by making the following eBook **FREE**!

To claim your free eBook, head over to

www.LivingAmongBigfoot.com

and click the "FREE BOOK" tab!

Report #3

My name's Gretchen, I'm now 49 and only recently moved away from the great city of New York, where the following bizarre occurrence took place. At the early age of 23, I was fortunate enough to get my hands on an internship over at Conde Nast. Ever since high school, it was a dream of mine to work for a major magazine, so when I received word shortly after graduating from The

University of Wisconsin, I was ecstatic. Luckily, a few of my sorority sisters were from New York City; never having been there before the move, one of them was able to connect me to a friend of theirs who was looking for a roommate.

The girl's name was Jen, and she resided in a surprisingly spacious two-bedroom apartment in Greenwich Village. Nowadays, it'd be nearly impossible to find anything like this for even a remotely affordable price; however, I suspect that her parents had a considerable share of wealth and were covering most of her living expenses during her postgrad years. I think her father might've even purchased the place; either way, I was obligated to give her a surprisingly small monthly check in exchange for the privilege of living in what quickly became my favorite city.

Jen was the quiet type, for the most part, usually keeping to herself and her daily obligations. She had a job as an event organizer that took up a substantial amount of her time, often having her travel to various locations during weekdays and weekends.

Most people at that age would agree how nice it is to have an entire apartment to yourself; maybe it was the size or the layout, but I admittedly felt a bit creeped out after sundown and especially when I'd be trying to fall asleep. It was an old building and was the stereotypical facility that you'd commonly see in a horror film, full of creaking floorboards, clanking pipes, etc.

I vividly remember watching TV at night while lying in my bed. It was, of course, before anything like Netflix existed; therefore, I was often bombarded with horror movie previews that blared through the speakers as I scrambled for the remote to change the channel or frantically closed my eyes while covering my ears. The last thing I ever wanted was to have the image of some ax-murderer or ghost embedded in my head while I was already consumed by the challenge of trying to doze off.

A few months had passed since I had moved to New York. Everything was running smoothly as I had settled into a routine; I had networked with a boatload of professionals within the industry while growing accustomed to my responsibilities within my respected office. I was lucky enough to make a good enough impression that the company decided to upgrade my previously unpaid internship into a paid assistant position. That was such a relief at the time because I was running low on money and was steadily approaching the point where I was going to have no choice but to ask my middle-class family for help. It was that or I figured out how to charge rent to a credit card.

Anyway, it was now winter, and Jen had just returned from a work trip that took place in the Caribbean (I know—brutal). I remember how I couldn't help but notice she was surprisingly pale for having spent four or five days under the tropical sun, however, we weren't close enough where I felt at all comfortable calling her out on something of the sort. This next part is going to sound incredibly strange, but it was that very same night as her return that she randomly came into my room around midnight, asking, in very few words, if she could sleep in my bed with me.

Having been woken up, I was a bit caught off guard, somewhat startled by the unexpected interaction. I couldn't help but perceive that her arms seemed to be quivering. I quickly moved over, making room so that she could get comfortable under the sheets. Of course, I immediately asked her what was wrong, but all she provided was a short response, crediting her current fluster to nothing more than a horrible night terror. It was before I could ask anything further that she appeared to have fallen asleep.

Jen had already departed for work when I awoke the next morning.

Her schedule was always quite sporadic compared to mine. I primarily worked a 10 am to 6 pm shift; meanwhile, she'd usually have to work weekends and was randomly given weekdays off; her workload seemed to fluctuate by the day. The previous night resonated with me as such an odd occurrence; Jen and I were friendly with one another, but at the end of the day, we were nothing more than roommates, having entirely different schedules, character, and friend circles. I would've always been up for hanging out with her, but I suppose I was just given the impression from early on that she wasn't all that interested, for whatever the reason might be. It's not like it offended me; after all, I was very aware that this is how many living situations were, especially within major cities. But that was what made the whole thing with Jen wanting to get into my bed so peculiar.

The next night played out in a nearly identical fashion. Again, with a tone of sympathy, I attempted to uncover what it was that was bothering her. But it was no use. It was if she was utterly drained once she'd arrive in my room, passing out within seconds of resting her head upon the pillow. This routine persisted for the next few days. My instinct was telling me not to pry, as I assumed that she'd talk to me when she was ready. For all I knew, she could've been dealing with someone recently having died, involvement in some sort of abusive relationship, or perhaps she was being forced to come to terms with underlying anxiety or depression that she couldn't make sense of. A week had passed since the beginning of this routine, and I was awoken around 1:30 am. Jen lay next to me in a deep sleep as I caught sight of the hallway light piercing through the little sliver of space that separated the floor from the door. I assumed that Jen must've gotten up in the middle of the night to use the bathroom but then forgot to turn it off on her way back into my bedroom. I was already a light sleeper as it was, so having any sort of shine beaming into my room made it near impossible to fall back asleep.

I was in the middle of scooching my body down the bed to get up when my eyes couldn't help but focus upon a bit of quick movement where the light emanated from. Given the fact that it was only the two of us who shared the apartment, I felt a knot in my throat. Still unfamiliar as to which of my floorboards triggered creaking noises, I hesitated to step off the bed so that I could reach for the telephone to call the police. I continued to sit atop the bed, desperately hoping that the intruder didn't notice the sound of my beating heart.

It then started to dawn on me how I couldn't hear any footsteps originating from outside the bedroom; if you had been inside this apartment, you would quickly realize how it would be impossible to sneak around the place. I remember scanning the room, looking for anything that I might be able to use as a weapon to defend myself; there was nothing. Internally panicking, and without any clue as to what I should do, I made the poor decision of nudging Jen until she woke up. Still half-asleep and disoriented, she raised her head to meet my eyes, desiring an explanation as to what was on my mind. As soon as I asked her if she had any friends staying over, I could've sworn her face went completely pale. She didn't even respond before she quickly swiveled her head to face the door.

It was that very instant she saw the light that she let out the most hair-raising scream of terror. She frantically leaped over my side of the bed, accidentally handing a knee smackdab in my ribs, as it was clear she wanted to get as far away from the door as possible. With her head down, she crouched in the corner, violently shaking as tears streamed down her face. With there now being close to no chance that whoever was there had not heard us, I rushed to grab the telephone before going over to join Jen in the corner. The emergency operator answered the call, but before I could even whisper a word, Jen let out another ear-piercing scream as we both witnessed what look like someone's feet float toward the middle of the space beneath the door.

The figure went still. It was as if it was observing the interior of the room even though the door was closed. The emergency operator could tell that we were distressed and immediately verified our address. She informed me that she had dispatched two officers to our location and that they'd arrive within a matter of minutes. Jen was now clinging to the side of my arm, burrowing her face into my shoulder. It was clear that she possessed an idea as to who was on the other side of that door. The whole thing was happening so fast that it left little time for us to discuss what was happening. Jen's persistent panic disallowed any communication as to what was going on. The figure continued to levitate in place, more than likely contemplating their next move. The dispatcher had remained on the other line, listening and softly inquiring for updates.

"Why would they be here? *Why* would *they* be here!?" Jen began to mutter while convulsing in my arms. With my sights still darting on that sliver of space beneath the door, I watched as the light from within the hallway suddenly went out. I carefully listened for any noise that could indicate the intruder's whereabouts, but aside from Jen, there was nothing. It couldn't have been more than a few minutes that passed before we heard assertive knocking upon the apartment's primary door, followed by a voice announcing it was the police. Due to the proximity of my bedroom to the front door, I gathered enough confidence to dash out of the bedroom and allow the officers into the apartment. Of course, part of me was frightened that someone could apprehend me before I made it to the door, but there was nobody there; there was only darkness. The officers were very kind. They thoroughly searched the place but were unable to locate any signs of a break-in. Still, I helped to file the police report while Jen mostly sat in silence. The officers assured us that our building would be monitored regularly and that it was okay for us to embrace a sense of safety.

After the police left, I nestled up next to Jen on the common area couch. In a caring but stern manner, I demanded that she told me exactly who she thought was out there and was responsible for so deeply terrifying her. She must've figured it was futile to avoid the subject. As she gazed at the floor, she went on to explain how she was "abducted" during her work trip in the Caribbean. Her memory of the incident was vague, although her fear was anything but.

I initially presumed that she was referring to kidnappers, or whatever other criminals were local to the land, but that was before mentioned tall, skinny, unclothed beings that she insisted were able to communicate with her via telepathy. My original instincts told me that perhaps she got sick and confused, thus imagining the entire event. However, it was difficult to disregard her genuine tone, as well as the tears. Whatever these things were, she claimed they didn't walk around like your average human; instead, they seemed to hover a few inches from the ground. It was pretty much impossible for me to develop any kind of rational explanation for the motion that took place just outside of the bedroom door, and that only made Jen's account even more credible.

Jen then explained that these odd-looking entities could illuminate their surroundings at will. It *did* dawn on me that the hallway light looked somehow different than the shine that emanated from a standard lightbulb; the best way I can describe it would be to say that it resembled the type of light that pierces through windows that face the sunrise. Of course, that was just my interpretation; for all I know, the

61

intruders could've utilized the hallway light switch. Much to shaken to go back to sleep, Jen and I stayed up for the remainder of that night, as I tried to avert her looming anxiety by discussing lighthearted things. Nothing out of the ordinary took place over the proceeding days, and soon, Jen went back to sleeping in her own bed. She eventually met a guy of which she ended up spending most of her time with when not working.

About six months later, I ended up being approached by a coworker (who had also become a close friend) who was moving into a cool new building that was a lot closer to my office. Since I was now making decent money, I took her up on the offer to lease one of the two-bedroom units. Jen and I continued to check in on one another for a few months but ultimately fell out of touch.

To this day, I still can't help but wonder if, on the other side of that door stood extraterrestrial life.

-Submitted by Gretchen G.

More Free Books at My Digital Store

If you're looking for NEW reads, check out my digital store
www.TomLyonsBooks.com.

Buying my books directly from me means you save money—because my store will always sell for less than big retailers. My store also offers sales, deals, bundles, and pre-order discounts you won't find anywhere else.

Visit my store now to check out exclusive books and other products not available anywhere else!

Report #4

I became a believer in extraterrestrial life following an incident in 2016. My wife and I both work as medical professionals around the Los Angeles area and have both worked many late shifts.

It was a somewhat chilly summer night as our schedules allowed for my wife and I to carpool home together. We were heading south on a road called *Old*

Topanga road and had only just driven past another side street with the name of *Valdez road*. It was sometime after 9:00 pm when the dark, winding road was briefly illuminated by numerous white, spherical lights that quickly but silently zipped from the rear of our vehicle, past the hood, and then seemingly faded into the horizon. I remember frantically slamming on the breaks since the rearview mirror initially presented an illusion that the strange lights were going to collide with our vehicle.

It's probably needless to say that we were both shocked by this occurrence. Being that it was 2016, my wife and I concluded that it must've been some sort of high-end drone that accidentally got too close to the roof of our car. Another strange aspect that I think is worth mentioning is that we observed one, maybe two other average-looking vehicles pass us while we were parked on the side of the road. Both of us always wondered whether those drivers had also spotted the same phenomenon.

After gathering our wits, we continued down the road, still debating an array of possible explanations. Then, no more than 60 seconds later, what we assumed to be the same lights appeared just to the right of our vehicle, almost as if they had teleported to the landscape along the side of the road. It was very dark at this time, but I was still able to discern what looked to be a black aircraft that was about maybe half the length of a typical commercial airplane. However, the thing appeared as though it could agilely move in any direction. I must say there was absolutely no sound to this machine; without the now seemingly dimmed lights, in relativity to the first sighting, I suspect that the thing could easily go undetected in various environments. I'm sure it sounds ridiculous, and it *was* possibly a figment of my imagination, but the object almost looked as if it was an *outline*, or even a mere *shadow*, as opposed to a solid object.

Later, my wife stated that the thing looked as if it were computer-generated or even miragelike. It all happened so fast, and due to justifiable astonishment, it's difficult to describe every detail accurately. What happened next was even more peculiar; our vehicle was still coasting, but as the craft quickly approached the point to where it was right above us, some kind of force caused us to stop suddenly. Now, judging by the particular road we were on, I'd estimate our speed to be somewhere between 25 and 35 mph. Considering that, one would have reason to believe the momentum from such a sudden halt would cause our bodies to lunge from our seats, but that wasn't the case. Instead, it was as if everything around us, including our bodies, came to an immediate but soft pause.

Just when you'd think things couldn't become any more perplexing, my wife and I both attest that we were overcome with calm, cool emotions... even as our vehicle had risen a few feet from the asphalt. Neither of us possesses any real recollection of what happened next, or even how long we were immersed in this tranquil state, but the whole thing felt undeniably surreal. At that moment, it never even occurred to

69

me that we should experience fear. The more I think back on it, the more it confuses me how I can't recall my wife ever shrieking from terror. Honestly, even though we vaguely remember finishing the drive home, we both concur that we didn't fully snap out of the hazy state until we were inside our house.

It didn't feel like a whole lot of time had passed, but I was utterly perplexed when I looked at the clock and recognized that nearly three hours had passed since we started the drive home. We have never been able to recollect what took place during those hours. Now, we avoid that route whenever possible. Years later, we came to learn that some of our closest friends had experienced something similar at a nearby location. I will reach out to them to see if they'd be willing to submit their story.

-Submitted by anonymous

Report #5

My name is Shayne, and I first want to mention how much I appreciate Max's interest in my experience. If more people like him took an interest in people's reports, we'd be a heck of a lot closer to disintegrating the government coverup. Believe me when I say it was a struggle to convince him to put this in here during our collaboration.

I live in a smaller-sized, industrial town known as Springfield, Ohio. The following event took place back in 2007, less than a week before my 35th birthday. The only reason I even remember that it was about to be my birthday was that I had a few friends in the area that I initially assumed to be messing with me but later came to realize that it would've been impossible for them to do so.

I was born and raised in Ohio, growing up in Dayton before eventually making the very short move over to Springfield not too long after finishing high school. I was connected to a family that managed multiple warehouse facilities throughout the Midwest and did this for a few years until the business expanded. With the workload rapidly growing, I was awarded the promotion to manage two of the facilities that were in Springfield. The man I had assisted moved over to Columbus, thus leaving an opening for me to take over what I was now highly experienced with.

Everything was smooth sailing for the next 15 or 16 years, easily having set into a somewhat simple routine. I want to mention that I never put much thought into aliens or martians, or whatever you prefer to call them. Aside from movies, videogames, and the occasional documentary, I just sort of assumed that if they had any contact with humans, we would all know about it by now.

I was working late one night, directing a handful of employees while they resituated some heavy machinery to create space for a new client. While in the front office of the facility, one of the

workers knocked on the door, bringing it
to my attention that there was an
unmarked crate that appeared delicate,
and they weren't sure what to do with it.
The only reason they even approached
me with the question, as opposed to
simply tossing it to the side, was because
they were very aware of how meticulous
I was when it came to organizing objects
within the warehouse. I always made it a
point to present to our customers just
how effective we were at making sure
their equipment was never at risk of
getting lost or facing damage.

The family who owns the
business was persistent in reminding the
managers that it was their caring
reputation that allowed the company to
become what it is today. While working
for a few years under the previous

manager, the detail-oriented approach became second nature.

I went out back to see the crate and was immediately confused as to who it could belong to. It certainly wasn't your typical style of packaging, having a simple or elegant chic vibe to it; the thing looked like something you'd come across in the film "Avatar", or something along those lines. There was no perceivable label of any kind, nor did it seem to match any of the other current inventory. I decided it would be best to leave the thing tucked away somewhere in the front office, as it was getting late, and I wanted to get going. If it were something of significant value, I'd soon receive notice of who the owner is and be able to figure out where it belongs.

After leaving the office that night, I didn't think much about it; it was incredibly rare, but I'd be lying if I said an item or two hadn't been misplaced in the past. Things would start to get very strange the next day. The following morning, I woke up early and went about my usual routine, consuming only black coffee and a slice of toast with butter and jam. After locking up my place, I was quick to notice that the windshield of my car was dowsed with what looked to be shaving cream. It was used to inscribe the sentence "Final Day of Early 30's". It was pretty lame, but one of my buddies who lived a few houses down was always making it apparent that he hadn't matured much since high school.

As usual, I arrived at the warehouse well before anyone else and was utterly shocked to behold that mysterious crate sitting there, opened, drenched with what looked to be blood. Though the scene was startling, I was overcome with a sigh of relief as I remembered the kind of friends I had. At the time, it was apparent to me that one of them had secretly arranged it with one of the employees to set up this whole "mystery crate" prank in the first place. Therefore, I began to carry on with the workday in a typical fashion, responding to emails, tracking payments, etc.

It wasn't long before the indulgence in coffee caused me to have to go to the restroom; upon washing my hands, I was startled by what my peripheral caught sight of in the mirror. At first glance, it appeared as though some kind of doll that portrayed a nude, short, and fragile person was lying on their stomach near the corner of the restroom. They were motionless, leading me to believe this was just another stupid trick; that was until I observed one of the elbows curve inward before whoever or *whatever* this thing was, scurried under one of the bathroom stalls. Being as how I was already close to the door, I frantically fled the restroom, having no clue as to what I had just seen. After having reentered the primary office, I snatched a nearby box cutter, inserting it into my pocket. Aside from the infrequent sound of the facility's old pipes, there was no noise.

I sat at my desk as my mind tried to dissect what that thing could've been. When I got up from my seat to take a closer look at the now opened crate, I used an old ruler to scrape at the interior walls of the sleek object. The bloodlike substance seemed to be already dried, but I thought I could detect a somewhat putrid stench emanating from the mess. By that point, I was almost convinced that I was on some hidden camera show or something like that. No offense to my friends, but this whole thing was far too intricate for them to orchestrate all on their own.

From the corner of my eye, I then noticed a tiny hand slowly reach under the doorway, in the direction of the crate, as if it was reaching for it. Again, baffled by the oddity of what I was seeing, I couldn't help but steadily back away; I was worried that the creature was going to slide its entire body under the door somehow. The thing wasn't at all intimidating in terms of size, but seeing as how quickly it moved frightened me in the sense that maybe it was venomous and could deliver a quick, lethal bite or something. I just had no clue what I was up against. I noticed my demeanor was frequently transitioning from being freaked out to trying to act tough when I reminded myself of the possibility that I was being recorded or monitored. I continued to stand there for maybe 20 seconds before the small hand withdrew itself from my sight.

Without further hesitation, I grasped my cellphone from my waistband and dialed my closest buddy's number. He answered after a couple of rings, sounding tired and presenting an impression that I had just woken him. He happily admitted that he and another friend were responsible for the shaving cream atop my windshield and that he committed the act in the middle of the night after a few hours at a local pub. But the guy acted as though he had no idea about what I was currently experiencing within the warehouse. I was still on the phone with him when I began to hear unfamiliar noises coming from the ceiling, sort of like what you'd expect to hear if a small animal had somehow found its way inside the ventilation system.

It was now at the point where I was genuinely scared, and I took the initiative to exit the building while calling the police. I knew it would be of no use to elaborate to them on what I had seen, so I decided to play the whole thing off as though there was an intruder inside the building. Two cops arrived within minutes.

After lighting up a cigarette, I stood outside for another five minutes before another squad car rolled up; this one an SUV. Two more gentlemen nodded in my direction as I pointed them toward the appropriate entrance. They didn't appear to be extraordinarily concerned.

Another 10 minutes had passed, and I was starting to become antsy, wondering whether I should reenter my office to see what the holdup was. I was stepping toward the side door when I crossed paths with the officers on their way out. One of the men informed me that they were unable to discern anyone, and if there was an intruder, they were long gone, and it was now safe for me to carry on with my routine. Slightly dumbfounded by the casualness of his words, I insisted that he follow me inside to see the strange crate that was soaked in the bloodlike substance. I led the way as he followed me into my office, only to be surprised that the mysterious object was no longer there. I pleaded with the guy that one of his fellow officers must've confiscated the item, but he was quick to shut that notion down, making it seem as though he had no knowledge of what I spoke of. Without the desire to argue, I eventually let it go and watched the police drive off.

Never again did I see any trace of the crate or the creepy humanoid that likely found its way out of it. I'd be lying if I were to say the whole incident didn't change my perspective on everything. Not a day goes by that I don't question whether the police were deliberately concealing whatever they were able to uncover during their time within the warehouse.

Or, perhaps whoever or *whatever* was responsible for placing the crate inside the warehouse, had repossessed the content before someone else could. I'm confident that I'll never uncover the truth.

-Submitted by Shayne N.

Report #6

Before my incident, I never thought much about extraterrestrial life. I was always interested whenever someone claimed to have seen something peculiar in the sky, as I *do* believe each of us possesses at least some level of curiosity about the subject matter. However, the topic was just never anything I cared to investigate myself. I suppose I was quite content with allowing the universe to naturally play its course and unravel these secrets to me, along with the rest of the population, whenever it felt ready.

I grew up in Phoenix, Arizona, where I spent most of my days playing sports, a somewhat even split between football and baseball. I eventually went on to play four years of college football and then was lucky enough to get drafted to the pros. I played for three different teams throughout five seasons before my career came to a sudden end due to injury. Frankly, I'd be fibbing if I were to tell you I was overwhelmingly disappointed. Shortly before my injury, I had already made up my mind that I'd only play one more season. As soon as I entered the league, I had made a pact with myself that I would be very diligent with any amount of money I'd accumulate from that point on. I witnessed so many horror stories where various other players seemed to be overtaken by dollar signs, immediately living their lives in a way that would make you think they had an orchid of money-growing trees within their backyard. I never really cared all that much for that celebrity "highlife" that so many people seem to desire. I think this perspective is something that my grandpa helped me to develop. I spent a lot of time with him while growing up. He was a bit of an alcoholic and had his own set of issues, but he did okay for himself financially speaking. He always made it a point to instruct me to "save, save, save!" and those words continue to reverberate through my brain to this very day.

After my professional career came to an end, I became attracted to the idea of moving out to Florida. The warm climate was appealing in the sense that it would be therapeutic for my achy joints. I also had the plan that I was going to purchase a nice boat and become an avid deep-sea fisherman. I was able to quickly find a modest-sized house right along the coast of the town known as Sarasota. Though I wasn't married yet, my girlfriend of four years didn't hesitate to move there with me. We were both excited about the change of scenery.

A little over a year passed since the relocation, and it felt as though we had made the right choice. One evening I had taken the boat out a few miles by myself to do some relaxing, solo fishing. It was nearly dark when I went inside the cabin to grab a beer from the small refrigerator. As I was using the bottle opener to remove the cap, I couldn't help but notice a tall, pale, longnecked being standing on the deck, gazing at me through the opened doorway. At that initial moment, I'm not sure I could've moved a single muscle, no matter how hard I tried.

-Submitted by Max Sanders

Conclusion

Thanks for reading! If you're looking for more, be sure to read *UFO Frightening Encounters, Volume 2.*

Editor's Note

Before you go, I'd like to say "thank you" for purchasing this book.

I know you had various books to choose from, but you took a chance at my content. Therefore, thanks for reading this one and sticking with it to the last page.

At this point, I'd like to ask you for a *tiny* favor; it would mean the world to me if you could leave a review wherever you purchased this book.

Your feedback will aid me as I continue to create products that you and many others can enjoy.

Mailing List Sign Up Form

Don't forget to sign up for the newsletter email list. I promise this will not be used to spam you, but only to ensure that you will always receive the first word on any new releases, discounts, or giveaways! All you need to do is visit the following URL and enter your email address.

http://eepurl.com/dhnspT

Social Media

Feel free to follow/reach out to me with any questions or concerns on either Instagram or Twitter! I will do my best to follow back and respond to all comments.

Instagram:

@living_among_bigfoot

Twitter:

@AmongBigfoot

About the Editor

A simple man at heart, Tom Lyons lived an ordinary existence for his first 52 years. Native to the great state of Wisconsin, he went through the motions of everyday life, residing near his family and developing a successful online business. The world that he once knew would completely change shortly after moving out west, where he was confronted by the allegedly mythical species known as Bigfoot.

You can email him directly at:

Living.Among.Bigfoot@gmail.com

Printed in Great Britain
by Amazon

35389218R00063